Stena Line
the **fleet**

Nick Widdows

Stena Line
Making good time™

Published by

Ferry Publications
PO Box 33, Ramsey, Isle of Man IM99 4LP
Tel: +44 (0) 1624 898446   Fax: +44 (0) 1624 898449
E-mail: ferrypubs@manx.net   Website: www.ferrypubs.co.uk

Stena Line Story

The he Stena Line story goes right back to 1939 when Sten Allan Olsson of Sweden formed a trading company. By 1946 this had developed into a scrap metal and manufacturing company and, with profits made, it was decided to venture into shipping. Until 1962 the company operated small coasters but in that year Sten formed Stena AB (taking his Christian name and the initial of his second name) and moved into passenger shipping, taking over Skagenlinjen AB and operating small passenger ships between Gothenburg and Skagen (and later Frederikshavn) in Denmark and also between Malmo and Kalstrup in Denmark. The ships were painted white with the familiar 'S' symbol on the red funnel - Stena Line was born.

The following year two car ferries - named the *Stena Danica* and *Stena Nordica* - were ordered from the shipyard at Le Trait in France. The plan was to operate the ships between Gothenburg and Frederikshavn but after the *Stena Danica* had entered service in 1965 it was found that traffic was not building up as much as was hoped and so the second ship went straight to a new service between Tilbury and Calais marketed as 'The Londoner'. This service was a moderate success but it was decided that the ship was too big and at the end of the summer season she was offered for sale. In the end she was not sold but instead chartered to British Rail to operate on their Stranraer - Larne route, where she remained until 1973. The

The *Stena Danica* opened the Gothenburg - Frederikshavn service in 1965 and she se

2

first stepping stone of the company's growth in the mid-1960s. *(Stena Line)*

Tilbury - Calais service resumed the following year but with the smaller *Prinsessan Christina*, chartered from rival operator Sessan Line.

In 1967 a new service to Kiel in North Germany was launched and a new ship - the Langesund-built *Stena Germanica* - was built for this route. A new, larger *Stena Danica* was delivered in 1969, replacing the older ship after only four years' service. By this time most of the coasters and small passenger vessels had been disposed of.

THE 1970s

In 1970 no less than four vessels were ordered from the yard at Trogir, Yugoslavia (now Croatia). Two were destined for the Gothenburg - Frederikshavn route to replace the almost brand-new *Stena Danica* whilst the other two were sold before delivery to Rederi AB Gotland - no doubt at a good profit - a typical Stena move! The third *Stena Danica* and running mate *Stena Jutlandica* were delivered in 1974 but by 1977 they too were considered too small and were enlarged to increase car capacity. Meanwhile on the Gothenburg - Kiel route a new *Stena Olympica* entered service in 1972, the year of the Munich Olympics and, as a running mate, the *Stena Scandinavica* entered service in 1973. The following year four ferries of a then unusual boxy design were delivered from Bremerhaven. The *Stena Nordica*, *Stena Normandica*, *Stena Nautica* and *Stena Atlantica* were not acquired for Stena Line service but for charter - and all have had very productive careers offering high capacity to the rapidly growing car and lorry ferry market both in Europe and world-wide.

3

The good-looking *Stena Germanica* pictured here during her first season in service. *(Stena Line)*

The *Koningin Beatrix* off Felixstowe inward-bound from Hook of Holland. *(Miles Cowsill)*

In 1983 Stena Line acquired Lion Ferry's operations between Grenaa and Varberg. Five years later Stena Line took full contol of Lion Ferry. The **Lion Prince**, pictured here, remained in the fleet until 1993 when she was replaced by larger tonnage. *(Ferry Publications Library)*

Although the purchase of passenger ships purely for charter was not repeated, in the 12-driver freight ferry market Stena has been a market leader. Although not operating many such routes themselves (currently the Gothenburg - Travemunde route is the only one) Stena ships and former Stena ships can be found all over the world on routes where the main traffic is trailers and containers on trailers. During the 1970s and early 1980s a bewildering array of ships was launched, some given Stena names and some given other names if the charter deal had been agreed before the launch. Most were sister ships, in several classes. First examples were the 1971-72 built *Stubbenkammer* (for Deutsche Reichbahn), *Anderida* (for British Rail) and *Stena Trailer* (which also went to British Rail as their

Dalriada after delivery). Between 1974 and 1977 came the 'Seaporter' class - the *Bison, Buffalo, Union Melbourne, Stena Tender, Stena Topper* and *Stena Timer*. Many of these ships have operated for Pandoro and later P&O Irish Sea and remain in service between Fleetwood and Larne, now operated by Stena Line. Then in 1977 and 1978 came the 11-strong Korean built 'Searunner' class with their distinctive 'oil tanker' style design - the *Alpha Enterprise, Atlantic Project, Atlantic Prosper, Elk, Imparca Empress, Merzario Ausonia, Merzario Espania, Norsky, Stena Runner, Stena Transporter* and *Tor Felicia*. All have different names now, some have been lengthened, some modified to ro-pax format and all, apart from the *Atlantic Prosper* which, as the *Finnbirch*, sank in a storm in November 2006, are still going strong.

In 1979 Stena Line launched an Oslo - Frederikshavn route using the former Swedish-Lloyd vessel, the 1966-built *Patricia*, which was renamed the *Stena Saga*.

THE 1980s

In 1980 a pooling agreement was reached with rival operator Sessan Line - Rederi AB Goteborg-Frederikshavn Linjen - whereby Stena took over the management of both companies' ships and a co-ordinated service was offered, branded as Stena-Sessan Line. Sessan Line had just taken delivery of a new large ferry for their Gothenburg - Frederikshavn service called the *Kronprinsessan Victoria*, which was to prove very useful for Stena Line in the ensuing years. Stena Line had placed orders for no less than six large ferries - two ships built in Dunkerque, France for the Gothenburg - Frederikshavn service to be delivered in 1982 and four night superferries to be built in Gdansk and Gdynia, Poland, to be delivered in 1983-84. Two would be used on the Gothenburg - Kiel route and the other two chartered out or used to develop new routes. Both deliveries experienced severe delays. The two French-built ships - the *Stena Danica* and *Stena Jutlandica* - were not delivered until 1983 and the situation regarding the Polish-built ships was even worse. Gdansk and Gdynia were the heartland of the Solidarnosc trade union movement and various industrial disputes were later compounded by the inability of the shipyards to pay for materials. Eventually, Stena Line purchased the first two ferries in their unbuilt state and paid for the necessary materials themselves, reimbursing the shipyards for the work only. The contract for the other two vessels was cancelled although the shipyard eventually sold both uncompleted hulls. The new *Stena Germanica* did not enter service until 1987 and the second ship, the *Stena Scandinavica,* did not arrive until 1988. Sessan Line's *Kronprinsessan Victoria* proved a godsend, initially on the Gothenburg - Frederikshavn route and then on the German route, with a vehicle deck fitted out with cabins. With the eventual delivery of the Polish ships she was transferred to the Oslo - Frederikshavn route and renamed the *Stena Saga*. Similarly Sessan Line's Gothenburg - Travemunde passenger ferry *Prinsessan Birgitta* was redeployed on Stena's Kiel route and renamed the *Stena Scandinavica*. The Travemunde route, which had a freighter on alternate days, became freight-only.

Work on Sessan Line's second ship was suspended for a time but she was eventually, in 1982, delivered as the new *Prinsessan Birgitta* and operated initially on the Gothenburg - Frederikshavn

The *Stena Britannica* arrives at the Hook of Holland on her maiden voyage following Stena Line purchasing her in 1991 for the UK-Dutch service. *(Ferry Publications Library)*

The *Stena Adventurer* is seen here leaving Holyhead in her last season on the Irish Sea in 1996. *(Miles Cowsill)*

The *Stena Explorer* leaving the shipyard for trials. *(Ferry Publications Library)*

route until the following year when she was modified in a similar way to her sister and chartered to British Rail Sealink where she became the *St Nicholas* on the Harwich - Hook of Holland service.

In 1982 Stena Line AB was renamed Stena AB and became the parent company to the Group. Stena Sessan Linjen AB was renamed Stena Line AB but continued to have outside shareholders and, from 1987, to be quoted on the Stockholm Stock Exchange. This situation continued until 2001 when the company returned to private ownership.

In 1988 Stena Line purchased Lion Ferry, which operated services between Grenaa in Denmark and Varberg in Sweden; at the same time, their Grenaa - Helsingborg service was acquired by DFDS. In 1987 Stena Line acquired control of all these services, re-launched the company with a new logo and livery and began giving the ships 'Lion' names. In 1989 they transferred the first *Stena Saga* to the route and renamed her the *Lion Queen*. A Grenaa - Halmstad service was introduced, which lasted until 1999.

During the 1980s both the British Rail ferry line Sealink UK Ltd and the Dutch carrier Stoomvaart Maatschappij Zeeland were privatised. In 1985 control of Sealink was gained by Sea Containers of Bermuda whilst, in 1989, Stena Line acquired the Dutch company which became Stena Line BV. Shortly after this purchase Stena Line began an intensive and sometimes acrimonious campaign to purchase Sealink and eventually, in 1990, the offer was such that the Sea Containers directors could no longer recommend shareholders other than acceptance. All of Sealink went to Stena except the ports of Folkestone, Newhaven and Heysham and the Isle of Wight operation.

THE 1990s

Stena Line entered the 1990s with a fleet which had almost doubled in size following the acquisition of Sealink UK Ltd from Sea Containers. It was a somewhat varied collection of vessels. Sealink had always had trouble under British Rail ownership in obtaining capital for investment, competing as they were with railway-related projects, and things were no better under Sea Containers' ownership, with new ships for the Isle of Wight only. Initially, the main change was in name from Sealink British Ferries to Sealink Stena Line, but the livery and logo devised immediately prior to privatisation were retained. Ships gradually received Stena names by the expedient of having the word 'Stena' placed before the previous name (eg. the *Hengist* became the *Stena Hengist*). Those ships named after saints received new names, often reviving historic railway ferry names but with the inevitable Stena prefix (eg *St Columba* became the *Stena Hibernia*). In 1993 a new livery was devised, still retaining the Sealink logo, but the trading name was changed to Stena Sealink Line. In 1996 the branding became 'Stena Line', using a new style that was applied throughout the fleet.

Having acquired Sealink, Stena Line set about updating the fleet. Two ro-pax ferries - the *Stena Challenger* and the *Stena Traveller* - had been ordered from the Fosen Yard in Norway and both were deployed on Sealink routes - the 'Challenger' first on Dover - Dunkerque, then Dover - Calais and finally on Holyhead - Dublin. The 'Traveller' also served on Holyhead - Dublin, a service Stena introduced to complement the Holyhead - Dun Laoghaire passenger service. The former DSB ferry *Peder Paars* was placed on

Stena Caledonia. (Nicholas Meads)

Stena Voyager. (Gordon Hislip)

the Dover - Calais route as the *Stena Invicta* and then, in 1996, the 1982-built *Stena Jutlandica*, replaced by a new vessel of the same name, joined the route as the *Stena Empereur*. On the Harwich - Hook of Holland route, the *St Nicholas* was replaced by the ex Silja Line vessel *Silvia Regina*, renamed the *Stena Britannica*, then later the former *Kronprinsessan Victoria*, which became the *Stena Europe*.

However, the greatest investment that Stena Line made in its new acquisition was the HSS project. The company started operating fast ferries in 1993 with the punningly-titled *Stena SeaLynx*, an Incat 74 metre craft introduced onto the Holyhead - Dun Laoghaire route. Two more similar but larger craft were chartered and at various times operated on the Dover - Calais, Newhaven - Dieppe and Fishguard - Rosslare routes. (The *Stena Lynx III* continues to operate that route). The HSS - High-speed Sea Service - is, however, in a different league. At 126m long by 40m wide, the three largest craft are almost twice as big as the earlier Incats and, with a service speed of 40 knots, about 5 knots faster . They were conceived in the early 1990s and construction began in 1994. The three all went to Stena Line's UK routes - Holyhead - Dun Laoghaire, Belfast - Stranraer and Harwich - Hook of Holland. With their higher speeds they were able to make more trips than conventional tonnage and faster crossing times were an obvious commercial attraction; in addition, unlike most other fast craft at the time they were able to take premium accompanied freight. Gas turbine power meant a lot of output for a low weight and no need for engine room staff, but this proved a major problem in the light of escalating oil prices in the next decade, especially for the high-grade fuel used by gas turbines.

The *Stena Jutlandica* was built for the Swedish-Danish route in 1996. She is pictured here being launched at her Dutch yard. *(Ferry Publications Library)*

The *Stena Challenger* entered service on the Dover operations during 1991 and later served on the Irish Sea. *(Miles Cowsill)*

Two smaller HSS craft were ordered from Westamarin of Kristiansand, Norway. Carrying 900 passengers compared with the larger craft's 1500, the first of these was delivered in 1997 as the *Stena Carisma* and placed on the Gothenburg - Frederikshavn service, but whilst the second vessel was in an early stage of construction the builders went into liquidation and all work ended. The partially completed hull of the second vessel was later scrapped.

The introduction of these revolutionary craft enabled further modernisation of the company's UK-based fleet. The two Harwich - Hook vessels were deployed elsewhere, the Dutch-flagged *Koningin Beatrix* to the Fishguard - Rosslare service and the *Stena Europe* to the Lion Ferry Karlskrona - Gdynia service as the *Lion Europe* (see below). On the Holyhead - Dun Laoghaire route, one ship was retained for the first summer - the *Stena Hibernia*, renamed the *Stena Adventurer* - with the *Stena Cambria* moved to the Dover - Calais service and on Stranraer - Belfast the *Stena Galloway* was sold and in the *Stena Antrim* moved to the Newhaven - Dieppe route.

In 1991 Stena Line inaugurated a new service between Southampton and Cherbourg, using the Harwich - Hook of Holland vessel the *St Nicholas*, renamed the *Stena Normandy*. The service ended in December 1996.

In 1992 Stena Line took over the loss-making Newhaven - Dieppe service from French railway company SNCF. The two ships operated - the *Champs Elysees* and *Versailles* (originally the third *Stena Danica*) - were renamed the *Stena Parisienne* and *Stena Londoner* respectively. Stena Line successfully raised standards on this rather 'down at heel' operation although profits continued to be difficult to obtain, especially after the opening of the Channel Tunnel in 1994.

All was not growth, however. In 1991 the Folkestone - Boulogne route was closed and the ships sold, and in 1993 ro-pax *Stena Challenger* was withdrawn from the Dover - Dunkerque route (although the French-operated train/lorry service continued until early 1996).

In 1998 the Dover and Newhaven operations of P&O European Ferries and Stena Line were merged as P&O Stena Line. Stena Line - which had a 40% share of the new company - contributed the *Stena Cambria, Stena Empereur, Stena Fantasia, Stena Invicta* and fast craft *Stena Lynx III*. The 'Invicta' did not operate for the new company and was subsequently sold. The *Stena Cambria* and *Stena Lynx III* operated for one season only at Newhaven, after which the route was closed. The fast craft, which had been renamed the *P&OSL Elite*, was then returned to Stena Line, resumed her previous name and since that time has operated between Fishguard and Rosslare.

In 1995 Stena Line moved into the Baltic with a service between Karlskrona and Gdynia in Poland, under the Lion Ferry name. Initially the route was operated by the 1967-built *Lion Queen* (formerly the *Stena Saga*) but traffic soon outgrew the vessel and the *Stena Europe* - as the *Lion Europe* - joined the route in 1997. In 1998 the Lion Ferry brand was dropped and the service was marketed as Stena Line, with the vessel reverting to the name of *Stena Europe*.

On Stena Line's traditional western Scandinavia routes there were less dramatic changes. In 1994 the *Stena Britannica* was transferred to the Oslo - Frederikshavn route and renamed the *Stena Saga*. As previously mentioned, a new Dutch-built *Stena Jutlandica*

Stena Danica. (FotoFlite)

was delivered in 1996. Sister ship of the *Stena Invicta*, the *Stena Nautica*, was deployed on the Lion Ferry Grenaa - Halmstad route as the *Lion King* between 1995 and 1996, then returned to the route in 1997 as the *Stena Nautica*.

In 1996 Stena ordered seven new ro-ro ships of modern design from Societa Esercizio Cantieri SpA of Viareggio, Italy for delivery in 1997 and 1998. They were known as the Stena 4Runner series and it was planned that some would be chartered to the British Royal Fleet Auxiliary to replace outdated tonnage. Unfortunately, in 1999 and well behind with the orders, the yard went into liquidation. One ship was nearly finished and was moved to another yard for completion and delivery. Two other ships were also in an advanced stage of completion but it took another four years before they were sold by auction - one going to an Italian company and completed in another Italian yard and the other purchased by Stena and completed in Croatia. Stena subsequently purchased the Italian owned vessel and both ships entered service as the *Stena Carrier* and *Stena Freighter* on the Gothenburg - Travemunde route in 2004.

In 1997 Stena AB purchased Sweferry AB (trading as Scandlines) from the Swedish State Railways. Renamed Scandlines AB, the company continued to operate separately from Stena Line.

THE 2000s

In 2000 the *Stena Nautica* was again transferred to the Varberg - Grenaa route, where she remains. During winter 2001-02 she was rebuilt to heighten her upper vehicle deck and allow separate loading of vehicle decks; her passenger capacity was reduced.

In 2001 Stena Line upgraded the Holyhead - Dublin route

through the charter of the new Italian Visentini Group ro-pax *Stena Forwarder*, replacing the *Stena Challenger* which was sold. She in turn was replaced two years later by the even larger *Stena Adventurer*. The ro-pax vessels on the Harwich - Hook of Holland route were also replaced in 2001 with the Spanish-built *Stena Britannica* and *Stena Hollandica*. In typical Stena style, the company actually ordered four ships but sold the first two to Finnlines before they were completed. The previously-operated freighters, with capacity for drivers, inaugurated a new service from Hook of Holland to Killingholme, near Immingham. Good traffic growth led to their replacement by new tonnage in 2006 and 2007. The 2001-built *Stena Britannica*, used on the evening service from the Hook, was replaced in 2003 by a new ship of the same name which gave extra capacity to this busy service. The older ship then joined her two near-sisters with Finnlines.

Stena Line's new route between Karlskrona and Gdynia showed remarkable growth in the few years it had operated and, by 2001, the *Stena Europe* was proving too small. Accordingly she swapped roles with the *Koningin Beatrix*, operating between Fishguard and Rosslare, this ship being renamed the *Stena Baltica*. Both ships received modifications to increase freight capacity, the *Stena Europe* having the extra cabins installed on the car deck twenty years earlier removed before entry onto the Irish route and the *Stena Baltica* having rather more complex modifications made in 2005. Additionally, in 2002 a second vessel was placed on the Polish route in the form of the 1992-built *Stena Traveller*. She was replaced in 2004 by the former P&O Irish Sea vessel *European Ambassador*, renamed the *Stena Nordica*. In 2007 a third vessel was added to the

Stena Nordica. *(Gordon Hislip)*

Gotaland. (Frank Lose)

The *Stena Felicity* replaced the *Stena Normandica* in 1990 on the Fishguard-Rosslare service. *(Miles Cowsill)*

Stena Line acquired the Fleetwood-Larne service in 2004. The *Stena Seafarer* with two other vessels currently maintains the link. *(Gordon Hislip)*

route in the form of the chartered *Finnarrow* from Finnlines.

Stena Line's joint venture with P&O on the Dover-Calais route came to an end in 2002, when P&O bought out the Stena Line share. At the same time, Stena Line took over P&O's three-ship Felixstowe - Rotterdam service, moving the UK terminal to Harwich after a few months. A similar arrangement took place on the Irish Sea in 2004, when Stena Line took over P&O's Fleetwood - Larne route and agreed both to move their North Channel operation in due course from Stranraer to the P&O port of Cairnryan and to abandon plans to build their own port in that location. Plans for Stena to take over P&O's Liverpool - Dublin service were blocked by the UK Office of Fair Trading on competition grounds, despite alternative services offered by Irish Ferries and Norse Irish Ferries.

In early 2007 Stena Line withdrew the HSS *Stena Discovery* from the Harwich - Hook of Holland service on economic grounds. High fuel costs had combined with a loss of passenger traffic due to the ending of duty-free sales and the growth of low-cost airlines. All traffic, including the carriage of foot passengers, was directed to the ro-pax ships which operated both day and night sailings. Both ships were lengthened during the first half of the year to bring them to about 240 metres long and additional cabins and other facilities were fitted. The second lengthened ship - the originally smaller *Stena Hollandica* - resumed service in May.

Following the debacle over the original Stena 4Runner ships in the 1990s, Stena ordered three improved versions of the same design from the Dalian shipyard in China. The Stena 4Runner Mark II ships were delivered in 2002 and 2003 and chartered out. New ro-pax ships for the Hook of Holland - Killingholme service - the *Stena*

Trader and *Stena Traveller* - were delivered in 2006 and 2007. They replaced the *Stena Searider* which was sold and the *Stena Seatrader* which moved to the Irish Sea to provide additional capacity on the Holyhead - Dublin route. Two more ships of similar design (but with an additional trailer deck) are due 2009. These are expected take over the Killingholme route with the existing vessels being moved to the Harwich - Rotterdam service, replacing the current 'Searunner' class vessels.

Late in 2006 Stena Line announced the order for two giant ro-pax ferries to be built in the Warnemunde and Wismar yards of Aker Yards (yards now owned by Waden Yards). The new *Stena Britannica* and *Stena Hollandica* will be 240m long and provide a staggering 5,500 lane metres for freight plus another 700 metres for cars. The 63,600t vessels are to be delivered in 2010 and will replace the existing ships on the Harwich - Hook route, which will be renamed and moved to the Karlskrona - Gdynia service.

In 2008, with continually rising oil prices, the decision was made to decelerate the two remaining UK HSS services between Holyhead and Dun Laoghaire and Stranraer and Belfast and reduce frequencies. In addition, a new terminal was opened at Belfast, nearer the mouth of Belfast Lough, reducing the length of the voyage by several miles. Plans to move to the P&O port at Cairnryan were scrapped due to escalating costs and other options are being examined. In the autumn the *Stena Nordica* was moved from the Karlskrona - Gdynia route to Holyhead - Dublin, replacing the *Stena Seatrader* and enabling four passenger services each way to be operated. In 2009 the Harwich - Rotterdam freight route was reduced to a two-ship service and the smaller *Stena Transporter* laid up.

The *Koningin Beatrix* was transferred to the Swedish-Polish route in 2002 and was renamed *Stena Baltica*. *(Jakub Bogucki)*

The *Stena Britannica* undergoing her jumboization at the German yard of Lloyd Werft. *(Ferry Publications Library)*

The *Stena Danica* leaves Gothenburg in January 2009 for Denmark on one of her regular daily sailings linking Sweden and Denmark. *(Bruce Peter)*

The *Stena Lynx III* maintains the seasonal fast ferry service between Fishguard and Rosslare. *(Gordon Hislip)*

2009 is going to be a difficult year for all operators, with the world-wide economic downturn affecting profits, but if any operator can weather the storm it will be Stena Line with their ability both to respond quickly and invest for the future.

STENA LINE TODAY

Stena Line is an international transport and travel services company, and one of the world's largest ferry operators. The Group has significant market shares in all its market sectors. This strong position is a result of strategic company acquisitions coupled with continual service and product development.

The Ferry Lines business area consists of Stena Line AB which is in three business areas: Scandinavia, North Sea and Irish Sea. Since 2000, the shipping company Scandlines AB has also been a wholly-owned subsidiary of Stena Line (see page 38).

The route network consists of 18 strategically-located ferry routes and four ports in Scandinavia and around the UK. The fleet consists of fast HSS ferries, traditional multi-purpose ferries, ro-pax ferries for passengers and freight, and ro-ro ferries for freight. Stena Line has in total around 5,700 employees, of whom around two-thirds are employed on board.

Stena Britannica. (FotoFlite)

FINNARROW

STENA ADVENTURER

Frank Lose

Gordon Hislip

	FINNARROW	STENA ADVENTURER
Gross Tons	25996	43532
Net:	7798	17935
Deadweight:	6124	9673
Length (m):	168.0	210.8
Breadth (m):	28.3	29.3
Draught (m):	6.6	6.3
Passengers:	200	1500
Cars:	800	-
Freight:	154 trailers (13.5m)	210 lorries (16m)
Year built:	1996	2003
Builders:	Pt Dok Kodja Bahri, Jakarta, Indonesia	Hyundai Heavy Industries, Ulsan, South Korea
Yard no:	1005	1393
Entered service with Stena	2007	2003
Engines:	4 x Sulzer 6ZA40S	2 x MAN-B&W/ 4 x Hyundai-B&W 9L40/54
Service Speed (knots):	21.0	22.5
Flag:	Sweden	United Kingdom
IMO Number:	9010814	9235529
Call Sign:	SMQE	VQLZ4
Usual Route:	Karlskrona-Gdynia	Holyhead-Dublin

STENA BALTICA

Jakub Bogucki

STENA BRITANNICA

FotoFilte

Stena Line the fleet

Gross Tons	31910
Net:	15170
Deadweight:	3060
Length (m):	164.6
Breadth (m):	27.6
Draught (m):	6.3
Passengers:	1800
Cars:	500
Freight:	45 trailers (13.5m)
Year built:	1986
Builders:	Van der Giessen-de Noord, The Netherlands
Yard no:	935
Year rebuilt:	2005
Entered service with Stena	1986
Engines:	MAN 8L40/45
Service Speed (knots):	20.0
Flag:	Bahamas
IMO Number:	8416308
Call Sign:	C6SK8
Usual Route:	Karlskrona-Gdynia
Former Names:	ex *Koningin Beatrix* 2002

Gross Tons	55050
Net:	24087
Deadweight:	11691
Length (m):	240.1
Breadth (m):	29.3
Draught (m):	6.3
Passengers:	900
Cars:	1311
Freight:	260 lorries (16m)
Year built:	2003
Builders:	Hyundai Heavy Industries, Ulsan, South Korea
Yard no:	1392
Year rebuilt:	2007
Rebuilders:	Lloyd Werft, Bremerhaven, Germany
Entered service with Stena	2002
Engines:	MAN-B&W
Service Speed (knots):	22.0
Flag:	United Kingdom
IMO Number:	9235517
Call Sign:	ZIYU5
Usual Route:	Harwich-Hook of Holland

23

STENA CALEDONIA

STENA CARISMA

Nicholas Meads

Miles Cowsill

	STENA CALEDONIA		STENA CARISMA
Gross Tons	12619	Gross Tons	8631
Net:	3652	Net:	2589
Deadweight:	2206	Deadweight:	480
Length (m):	129.6	Length (m):	88.0
Breadth (m):	21.6	Breadth (m):	30.0
Draught (m):	4.8	Draught (m):	4.8
Passengers:	1000	Passengers:	900
Cars:	280	Cars:	210
Freight:	56 lorries (16m)	Freight:	-
Year built:	1981	Year built:	1997
Builders:	Harland & Wolff Ltd, Belfast, UK	Builders:	Westamarin A/S, Kristiansand, Norway
Yard no:	1717	Yard no:	238
Entered service with Stena	1981	Entered service with Stena	1997
Engines:	2 x Pielstick-Crossley 16PC2V Mk5	Engines:	2 x ABB Stal GT-35 gas turbine
Service Speed (knots):	19.5	Service Speed (knots):	40.0
Flag:	United Kingdom	Flag:	Sweden
IMO Number:	7910917	IMO Number:	9127760
Call Sign:	GBZY	Call Sign:	SGFV
Usual Route:	Stranraer- Belfast	Usual Route:	Gothenburg-Frederikshavn
Former Names:	ex *St David* 1990		

STENA CARRIER

Nick Widdows

STENA DANICA

Miles Cowsill

Gross Tons	21089	Gross Tons	28727
Net:	7800	Net:	8061
Deadweight:	12350	Deadweight:	2950
Length (m):	182.6	Length (m):	154.9
Breadth (m):	25.5	Breadth (m):	28.3
Draught (m):	7.4	Draught (m):	6.3
Passengers:	12	Passengers:	2274
Freight:	200 trailers (13.5m)	Cars:	555
Year built:	2004	Freight:	120 trailers (13.5m)
Builders:	Societa Esercizio Cantieri SpA, Viareggio. Italy	Year built:	1983
Yard no:	1548	Builders:	Ch du Nord et de la Mediterranee, Dunkerque,
Year rebuilt:	2004 (completion)		France
Rebuilders:	Nuovi Cantieri Apuania, La Spezia, Italy	Yard no:	309
Entered service with Stena	2004	Entered service with Stena	1983
Engines:	4 x Sulzer 8ZA40S	Engines:	4 x Sulzer 12ZV40
Service Speed (knots):	22.0	Service Speed (knots):	19.5
Flag:	Sweden	Flag:	Sweden
IMO Number:	9138800	IMO Number:	7907245
Call Sign:	SBFG	Call Sign:	SKFH
Usual Route:	Gothenburg-Travemunde	Usual Route:	Gothenburg-Frederikshavn
Former Names:	ex *Aronte* 2004, *Stena Carrier II* 2004		

STENA EUROPE

Gordon Hislip

STENA EXPLORER

Gordon Hislip

	STENA EUROPE		STENA EXPLORER
Gross Tons	24828	Gross Tons	19638
Net:	7859	Net:	5891
Deadweight:	3315	Deadweight:	1500
Length (m):	149.0	Length (m):	126.6
Breadth (m):	26.6	Breadth (m):	40.0
Draught (m):	6.1	Draught (m):	4.8
Passengers:	2076	Passengers:	1500
Cars:	456	Cars:	375
Freight:	60 trailers (13.5m)	Freight:	50 lorries (16m)
Year built:	1981	Year built:	1996
Builders:	Gotaverken Arendal AB, Gothenburg, Sweden	Builders:	Finnyards, Rauma, Finland
Yard no:	908	Yard no:	404
Entered service with Stena	1981	Entered service with Stena	1996
Engines:	4 x Fyra Nohab-Wartsila Vasa 12V32A	Engines:	2 x General Electric LM 2500/ 2 x General Electric LM 1600 Gas Turbines
Service Speed (knots):	19.0	Service Speed (knots):	40.0
Flag:	United Kingdom	Flag:	United Kingdom
IMO Number:	7901760	IMO Number:	9080194
Call Sign:	VSTA3	Call Sign:	MVBD8
Usual Route:	Fishguard- Rosslare	Usual Route:	Holyhead-Dun Laoghaire
Former Names:	ex *Kronprinsessan Victoria* 1994, *Stena Saga* 1994, *Stena Europe* 1997, *Lion Europe* 1998		

STENA FREIGHTER

STENA GERMANICA

Miles Cowsill

	STENA FREIGHTER		STENA GERMANICA
Gross Tons	21104	Gross Tons	39178
Net:	7800	Net:	22089
Deadweight:	12350	Deadweight:	4000
Length (m):	182.6	Length (m):	175.4
Breadth (m):	25.5	Breadth (m):	30.8
Draught (m):	7.4	Draught (m):	6.7
Passengers:	12	Passengers:	2400
Freight:	200 trailers (13.5m)	Cars:	550
Year built:	2004	Freight:	120 trailers (13.5m)
Builders:	Societa Esercizio Cantieri SpA, Viareggio. Italy	Year built:	1987
Yard no:	1547	Builders:	Gdynia Stocznia i Komuni Paryski, Gdynia, Poland
Year rebuilt:	2004 (completion)		
Rebuilders:	Brodogradiliste Kraljevica, Croatia	Yard no:	B494/1
Entered service with Stena	2004	Entered service with Stena	1987
Engines:	4 x Sulzer 8ZA40S	Engines:	4 x Zgoda-Sulzer 16ZV49/48
Service Speed (knots):	22.0	Service Speed (knots):	20.0
Flag:	Sweden	Flag:	Sweden
IMO Number:	9138795	IMO Number:	7907659
Call Sign:	SJRX	Call Sign:	SKPZ
Usual Route:	Gothenburg-Travemunde	Usual Route:	Gothenburg-Kiel
Former Names:	ex *Sea Chieftain* 2003, *Stena Seafreighter* 2004		

STENA HOLLANDICA

STENA JUTLANDICA

Frank Lose

FotoFlite

Gross Tons	44372
Net:	17209
Deadweight:	11378
Length (m):	240.1
Breadth (m):	28.7
Draught (m):	6.2
Passengers:	900
Cars:	1290
Freight:	250 lorries (16m)
Year built:	2001
Builders:	Astilleros Espanoles, Puerto Real, Spain
Yard no:	81
Year rebuilt:	2007
Rebuilders:	Lloyd Werft, Bremerhaven, Germany
Entered service with Stena	2001
Engines:	4 x Sulzer 8ZAL40S
Service Speed (knots):	22.0
Flag:	The Netherlands
IMO Number:	9145176
Call Sign:	PFBL
Usual Route:	Harwich-Hook of Holland

Gross Tons	29691
Net:	9046
Deadweight:	6300
Length (m):	183.7
Breadth (m):	28.4
Draught (m):	6.0
Passengers:	1500
Cars:	550
Freight:	156 trailers (13.5m)
Year built:	1996
Builders:	Van der Giessen-de Noord, Krimpen aan den IJssel, The Netherlands
Yard no:	967
Entered service with Stena	1996
Engines:	4 x MAN B&W 9L48/54
Service Speed (knots):	21.5
Flag:	Sweden
IMO Number:	9125944
Call Sign:	SEAN
Usual Route:	Gothenburg-Frederikshavn
Former Names:	ex *Stena Jutlandica III* 1996

STENA LEADER

Matthew Davies

Gross Tons	12879
Net:	1171
Deadweight:	5805
Length (m):	157.2
Breadth (m):	19.1
Draught (m):	3.8
Passengers:	50
Freight:	114 trailers (13.5m)
Year built:	1975
Builders:	J J Sietas KG Schiffswerke GmbH & Co, Hamburg, Germany
Yard no:	756
Entered service with Stena	2004
Engines:	2 x Klockner-Humboldt-Deutz RBV12M540
Service Speed (knots):	17.0
Flag:	Bermuda
IMO Number:	7361582
Call Sign:	ZCBF8
Usual Route:	Fleetwood-Larne
Former Names:	ex *Buffalo* 1998, *European Leader* 2004

STENA LYNX III

Godon Hislip

Gross Tons	4113
Net:	1745
Deadweight:	310
Length (m):	81.1
Breadth (m):	26.0
Draught (m):	3.1
Passengers:	620
Cars:	181
Year built:	1996
Builders:	Incat, Hobart, Australia
Yard no:	040
Entered service with Stena	1996
Engines:	4 x 16-cyl Ruston
Service Speed (knots):	35.0
Flag:	Bahamas
IMO Number:	9129328
Call Sign:	C6NU2
Usual Route:	Fishguard- Rosslare
Former Names:	ex *Stena Lynx III* 1998, *Elite* 1998, *P&O Stena Elite* 1998, *Stena Lynx III* 2003, *Elite* 2004

StenaLine the fleet

STENA NAUTICA

Miles Cowsill

STENA NORDICA

Gordon Hislip

Gross Tons	19504
Net:	6154
Deadweight:	2813
Length (m):	134.0
Breadth (m):	24.6
Draught (m):	5.6
Passengers:	700
Cars:	330
Freight:	70 trailers (13.5m)
Year built:	1986
Builders:	Nakskov Skipsvaerft A/S, Nakskov, Denmark
Yard no:	234
Year rebuilt:	2001
Rebuilders:	Oresundsvarvet AB, Landskrona, Sweden
Entered service with Stena	1995
Engines:	2 x B&W 8L45GB
Service Speed (knots):	19.4
Flag:	Sweden
IMO Number:	8317954
Call Sign:	SGQU
Usual Route:	Varberg-Grenaa
Former Names:	ex *Niels Klim* 1990, *Stena Nautica* 1992, *Isle of Innisfree* 1995, *Lion King* 1996

Gross Tons	24206
Net:	12201
Deadweight:	4884
Length (m):	169.8
Breadth (m):	25.8
Draught (m):	6.0
Passengers:	405
Cars:	375
Freight:	122 trailers (13.5m)
Year built:	2001
Builders:	Mitsubishi Heavy Industries, Shimonoseki, Japan
Yard no:	1068
Entered service with Stena	2004
Engines:	2 x Wartsila 18V38, 2 x Wartsila 12V38
Service Speed (knots):	25.0
Flag:	British as from April 2009
IMO Number:	9215505
Call Sign:	SCBK
Usual Route:	Karlskrona-Gdynia
Former Names:	ex *European Ambassador* 2004

STENA PARTNER

Nick Widdows

Gross Tons	21162
Net:	6348
Deadweight:	6594
Length (m):	184.9
Breadth (m):	23.5
Draught (m):	6.4
Passengers:	166
Freight:	180 trailers (13.5m)
Year built:	1977
Builders:	Hyundai Shipbuilders & Heavy Industries, S Korea
Yard no:	649
Year rebuilt:	1981
Rebuilders:	Lloyd Werft GmbH, Bremerhaven, Germany
Entered service with Stena	2002
Engines:	2 x Pielstick 12PC2-5V-400 V
Service Speed (knots):	16.5
Flag:	United Kingdom
IMO Number:	7528635
Call Sign:	GFWR
Usual Route:	Harwich-Rotterdam
Former Names:	ex *Alpha Enterprise* 1970, *Syria* 1983, *Stena Transporter* 1986, *Cerdic Ferry* 1992, *European Freeway* 2002, *Freeway* 2002

STENA PIONEER

Trevor Kidd

Gross Tons	14426
Net:	1103
Deadweight:	5805
Length (m):	141.8
Breadth (m):	22.0
Draught (m):	4.7
Passengers:	96
Freight:	114 trailers (13.5m)
Year built:	1975
Builders:	J J Sietas KG Schiffswerke GmbH & Co, Hamburg, Germany
Yard no:	755
Year rebuilt:	1995
Rebuilders:	Cammel Laird, Birkenhead, England
Entered service with Stena	2004
Engines:	2 x Klöckner-Humboldt-Deutz 12M540
Service Speed (knots):	16.0
Flag:	Bermuda
IMO Number:	7361570
Call Sign:	ZCBJ8
Usual Route:	Fleetwood-Larne
Former Names:	ex *Bison* 1997, *European Pioneer* 2004

STENA SAGA

FotoFlite

STENA SCANDINAVICA

Miles Cowsill

	STENA SAGA		STENA SCANDINAVICA
Gross Tons	33750	Gross Tons	39169
Net:	14015	Net:	14786
Deadweight:	3898	Deadweight:	4500
Length (m):	166.1	Length (m):	175.4
Breadth (m):	28.5	Breadth (m):	31.0
Draught (m):	6.7	Draught (m):	6.8
Passengers:	2000	Passengers:	2400
Cars:	510	Cars:	550
Freight:	76 trailers (13.5m)	Freight:	120 trailers (13.5m)
Year built:	1981	Year built:	1988
Builders:	Oy Wartsila AB, Turku, Finland	Builders:	Stocznia im Lenina, Gdansk, Poland
Yard no:	1252	Yard no:	B494/2
Entered service with Stena	1991	Entered service with Stena	1988
Engines:	2 x Wartsila-Pielstick 12PC2,5V	Engines:	4 x Zgoda-Sulzer 16ZV49/48
Service Speed (knots):	22.0	Service Speed (knots):	20.0
Flag:	Sweden	Flag:	Sweden
IMO Number:	7911545	IMO Number:	7907661
Call Sign:	SLVH	Call Sign:	SLYH
Usual Route:	Oslo-Frederikshavn	Usual Route:	Gothenburg-Kiel
Former Names:	ex *Silvia Regina* 1991, *Stena Britannica* 1994		

STENA SCANRAIL

Nick Widdows

STENA SEAFARER

Godon Hislip

Gross Tons	7504
Net:	2251
Deadweight:	6726
Length (m):	142.4
Breadth (m):	19.1
Draught (m):	5.9
Passengers:	65
Freight:	64 trailers (13.5m) and/or rail wagons
Year built:	1973
Builders:	Van der Giessen-de Noord, The Netherlands
Yard no:	863
Year rebuilt:	1987
Rebuilders:	Cityvarvet, Gothenburg
Entered service with Stena	1987
Engines:	2 x Werkspoor-Amsterdam TM 410
Service Speed (knots):	16.5
Flag:	Sweden
IMO Number:	7305772
Call Sign:	SLBM
Usual Route:	Gothenburg-Frederikshavn
Former Names:	ex *Stena Seatrader* 1973, *Seatrader* 1976, *Bahjan* 1981, *Stena Searider* 1983, *Searider* 1984, *Stena Searider* 1984, *Trucker* 1985, *Stena Searider* 1987

Gross Tons	10957
Net:	3287
Deadweight:	4020
Length (m):	141.8
Breadth (m):	19.4
Draught (m):	4.7
Passengers:	50
Freight:	80 trailers (13.5m)
Year built:	1975
Builders:	J J Sietas KG Schiffswerke GmbH & Co, Hamburg, Germany
Yard no:	757
Year rebuilt:	1975
Rebuilders:	Nobiskrug Werft GmbH, Rendsburg, Germany
Entered service with Stena	2004
Engines:	2 x Klockner-Humboldt-Deutz 12M540
Service Speed (knots):	18.0
Flag:	Bermuda
IMO Number:	7361594
Call Sign:	ZCAZ2
Usual Route:	Fleetwood-Larne
Former Names:	ex *Union Melbourne* 1980, *Puma* 1998, *European Seafarer* 2004

33

STENA TRADER

Henk van der Lugt

Gross Tons	26663
Net:	12110
Deadweight:	7500
Length (m):	212.5
Breadth (m):	26.7
Draught (m):	6.3
Passengers:	300
Freight:	220 trailers (13.5m)
Year built:	2006
Builders:	Fosen Mekaniske Verksted, Rissa, Norway
Yard no:	74
Entered service with Stena	2006
Engines:	2 x B&W MAN 9L48/60B
Service Speed (knots):	22.2
Flag:	The Netherlands
IMO Number:	9331177
Call Sign:	PHGC
Usual Route:	Killingholme-Hook of Holland (to move to Harwich-Rotterdam in 2011)

STENA TRANSFER

Nick Widdows

Gross Tons	21162
Net:	6348
Deadweight:	6594
Length (m):	184.9
Breadth (m):	23.5
Draught (m):	6.4
Passengers:	166
Freight:	180 trailers (13.5m)
Year built:	1977
Builders:	Hyundai Shipbuilders & Heavy Industries, Ulsan, South Korea
Yard no:	643
Entered service with Stena	2002
Engines:	2 x Pielstick 12PC2-5V-400
Service Speed (knots):	16.0
Flag:	United Kingdom
IMO Number:	7528570
Call Sign:	GFVM
Usual Route:	Harwich-Rotterdam
Former Names:	ex *Stena Runner* 1977, *Alpha Progress* 1979, *Hellas* 1986, *Doric Ferry* 1992, *European Tideway* 2002, *Ideway* 2002

STENA TRANSPORTER

Gordon Hislip

Gross Tons	16776
Net:	5032
Deadweight:	5087
Length (m):	151.0
Breadth (m):	23.5
Draught (m):	6.5
Passengers:	74
Freight:	122 trailers (13.5m)
Year built:	1978
Builders:	Hyundai Shipbuilders & Heavy Industries, Ulsan, South Korea
Yard no:	651
Entered service with Stena	2002
Engines:	2 x Pielstick 12PC2-5V-400
Service Speed (knots):	17.0
Flag:	United Kingdom
IMO Number:	7528659
Call Sign:	GZOL
Usual Route:	Laid up
Former Names:	ex *Merzario Espania* 1978, *Merzario Hispania* 1979, *Nordic Ferry* 1992, *Pride of Flanders* 2002, *Flanders* 2002

STENA TRAVELLER

Nick Widdows

Gross Tons	26663
Net:	12110
Deadweight:	7500
Length (m):	212.5
Breadth (m):	26.7
Draught (m):	6.3
Passengers:	300
Freight:	220 trailers (13.5m)
Year built:	2007
Builders:	Fosen Mekaniske Verksted, Rissa, Norway
Yard no:	75
Entered service with Stena	2007
Engines:	2 x MAN B&W 9L48/60B
Service Speed (knots):	22.2
Flag:	The Netherlands
IMO Number:	9331189
Call Sign:	PHJU
Usual Route:	Killingholme-Hook of Holland (to move to Harwich-Rotterdam in 2011)

STENA VOYAGER

Gordon Hislip

STENA BRITANNICA

Gross Tons	19638
Net:	5892
Deadweight:	1500
Length (m):	126.6
Breadth (m):	40.0
Draught (m):	4.8
Passengers:	1500
Cars:	375
Freight:	50 lorries (16m)
Year built:	1996
Builders:	Finnyards, Rauma, Finland
Yard no:	405
Entered service with Stena	1996
Engines:	2 x General Electric LM 2500/ 2 x General Electric LM 1600 Gas Turbines
Service Speed (knots):	40.0
Flag:	United Kingdom
IMO Number:	9080209
Call Sign:	MWJH3
Usual Route:	Stranraer- Belfast

Gross Tons	63600
Net:	-
Deadweight:	11600
Length (m):	240.0
Breadth (m):	32.0
Draught (m):	6.4
Passengers:	1200
Cars:	-
Freight:	300 trailers (13.5m)
Year built:	2010
Builders:	Waden Yards, Warnemunde & Wismar
Yard no:	159
Engines:	4 x MAN 48/60CR
Service Speed (knots):	22.0
Flag:	-
IMO Number:	-
Call Sign:	-
Planned Route:	Harwich-Hook of Holland

Stena Line

Stena Line

Gross Tons	63600
Net:	-
Deadweight:	11600
Length (m):	240.0
Breadth (m):	32.0
Draught (m):	6.4
Passengers:	1200
Cars:	-
Freight:	300 trailers (13.5m)
Year built:	2010
Builders:	Waden Yards, Warnemunde & Wismar
Yard no:	164
Engines:	4 x MAN 48/60CR
Service Speed (knots):	22.0
Flag:	-
IMO Number:	-
Call Sign:	-
Planned Route:	Harwich-Hook of Holland

Gross Tons	37500
Net:	-
Deadweight:	8500
Length (m):	212.0
Breadth (m):	26.7
Draught (m):	6.3
Passengers:	300
Freight:	290 trailers (13.5m)
Year built:	2011
Builders:	Samsung Heavy Industries, Koje, South Korea
Yard no:	1807
Engines:	2 x MAN 21600
Service Speed (knots):	23.0
Flag:	-
IMO Number:	-
Call Sign:	-
Planned Route:	Hook of Holland-Killingholme

SCANDLINES AB

Scandlines AB of Sweden is a wholly owned subsidiary of Stena Line. The company, previously owned by Statens Järnvägar (Swedish State Railways), was purchased by Stena Line in 2000. All routes - except the Trelleborg - Travemünde freight only service - operated by Scandlines AB are joint with Scandlines GmbH, a company privatised in 2007 and now owned by Danish, German and UK interests.

Address: Scandlines AB, Knutpunkten 43
252 78 Helsingborg, Sweden
Tel: +46 42-18 60 00   Fax:+46 (0)42-18 60 49

AURORA AF HELSINGBORG

Miles Cowsill

Gross Tons	10918
Net:	3275
Deadweight:	2300
Length (m):	111.2
Breadth (m):	28.2
Draught (m):	5.5
Passengers:	1250
Cars:	225
Freight:	25 lorries (16m)
Year built:	1992
Builders:	Langsten Verft A/S, Tomrefjord, Norway
Yard no:	157
Engines:	4 x Wartsila-Vasa 6R32E
Service Speed (knots):	14.0
Flag:	Sweden
IMO Number:	9007128
Call Sign:	SCQX
Usual Route:	Helsingborg-Helsingor

GOTALAND

Stena Line

Gross Tons	18060
Net:	9708
Deadweight:	5209
Length (m):	183.1
Breadth (m):	22.5
Draught (m):	5.8
Passengers:	400
Cars:	230
Freight:	102 trailers (13.5m)
Year built:	1973
Builders:	A/S Nakskov Skipsvaerft, Nakskov, Denmark
Yard no:	198
Years rebuilt:	1992 and 1994
Rebuilders:	Oresundsvarvet AB, Landskrona, Sweden
Engines:	4 x Lindholmen-Pielstick PC2L-400
Service Speed (knots):	17.2
Flag:	Sweden
IMO Number:	7229514
Call Sign:	SEAU
Usual Route:	Trelleborg-Travemunde

SKANE

TRELLEBORG

FotoFlite

Frank Lose

Gross Tons	42705
Net:	21731
Deadweight:	7290
Length (m):	200.2
Breadth (m):	29.6
Draught (m):	6.5
Passengers:	600
Cars:	520
Freight:	240 trailers (13.5m)
Year built:	1998
Builders:	Astilleros Espanoles, Puerto Real, Spain
Yard no:	77
Engines:	4 x MAN-B&W 48/60L8
Service Speed (knots):	21.0
Flag:	Sweden
IMO Number:	9133915
Call Sign:	SIEB
Usual Route:	Trelleborg-Rostock

Gross Tons	20028
Net:	6471
Deadweight:	3800
Length (m):	170.2
Breadth (m):	23.8
Draught (m):	5.8
Passengers:	900
Cars:	900
Freight:	90 trailers (13.5m)
Year built:	1981
Builders:	Oresundsvarvet AB, Landskrona, Sweden
Yard no:	271
Engines:	4 x MAN 8L40/45
Service Speed (knots):	21.0
Flag:	Sweden
IMO Number:	7925297
Call Sign:	SIZM
Usual Route:	Trelleborg-Sassnitz

Stena Foreteller. (Anders Woerteler)

STENA RORO

Stena RoRo is a wholly owned subsidiary of Stena AB. Its fleet consists of ro-ro and ro-pax vessels which are time - or bare-boat - chartered to customers world-wide. Stena RoRo also works as an in house supplier of vessels to Stena Line; vessels owned by Stena RoRo and operated by Stena Line are listed under Stena Line.

Address: Stena RoRo, 405 19 Gothenburg ,Sweden

Tel: +46 31 85 50 00   Fax: +46 31 85 50 55

ARK FORWARDER

Kai Ortel

Gordon Hislip

Gross Tons	21104
Net:	7800
Deadweight:	12350
Length (m):	182.6
Breadth (m):	25.5
Draught (m):	7.4
Passengers:	12
Freight:	196 trailers (13.5m)
Year built:	1998
Builders:	Societa Esercizio Cantieri SpA, Viareggio, Italy
Yard no:	1546
Engines:	4 x Sulzer 8ZA40S
Service Speed (knots):	22.0
Flag:	United Kingdom
IMO Number:	9138783
Call Sign:	GDIW
Operator:	DFDS Tor Line
Former Names:	ex *Stena Ausonia* 1998, *Sea Centurion* 2003, *Mont Ventoux* 2005, *Stena Forwarder* 2007

BORJA

Bruce Peter

Gross Tons	26500
Net:	7500
Deadweight:	7000
Length (m):	186.5
Breadth (m):	25.6
Draught (m):	6.6
Passengers:	1000
Freight:	160 trailers (13.5m)
Year built:	2007
Builders:	CN Visentini di Visentini Francesco & C, Donada, Italy
Yard no:	216
Engines:	2 x MAN B&W
Service Speed (knots):	24.0
Flag:	Italy
IMO Number:	9349760
Call Sign:	ICEC
Operator:	Eurolineas Maritimas SA
Former Names:	ex Stena Ausonia 2007

MONT VENTOUX

Frank Lose

Gross Tons	18469
Net:	5540
Deadweight:	13364
Length (m):	183.1
Breadth (m):	25.2
Draught (m):	7.8
Passengers:	12
Freight:	144 trailers (13.5m)
Year built:	1996
Builders:	CN Visentini di Visentini Francesco & C, Donada, Italy
Yard no:	170
Engines:	MAN-B&W 8L 58/64
Service Speed (knots):	19.7
Flag:	United Kingdom
IMO Number:	9129586
Call Sign:	MGTT6
Operator:	Sudcargo
Former Names:	ex Lindarosa 2005

STENA DISCOVERY

STENA FORECASTER

FotoFlite

Sebastian Ziehl

Gross Tons	19638
Net:	5891
Deadweight:	1500
Length (m):	126.6
Breadth (m):	40.0
Draught (m):	4.8
Passengers:	1500
Cars:	375
Freight:	50 lorries (16m)
Year built:	1997
Builders:	Finnyards, Rauma, Finland
Yard no:	406
Entered service with Stena	1997
Engines:	2 x General Electric LM 2500/ 2 x General Electric LM 1600 Gas Turbines
Service Speed (knots):	40.0
Flag:	The Netherlands
IMO Number:	9107590
Call Sign:	PCCU
Operator:	Laid up

Gross Tons	24688
Net:	7407
Deadweight:	12300
Length (m):	195.3
Breadth (m):	26.8
Draught (m):	6.6
Passengers:	12
Freight:	210 trailers (13.5m)
Year built:	2003
Builders:	Dalian Shipyard, Dalian, China
Yard no:	RO123-2
Engines:	4 x Sulzer 8ZAL40S
Service Speed (knots):	22.5
Flag:	Sweden
IMO Number:	9214678
Call Sign:	SCKZ
Operator:	Transfennica, Finland

STENA FORERUNNER

Sebastian Ziehl

Gross Tons	24688
Net:	7407
Deadweight:	12300
Length (m):	195.3
Breadth (m):	26.8
Draught (m):	6.6
Passengers:	12
Freight:	210 trailers (13.5m)
Year built:	2002
Builders:	Dalian Shipyard, Dalian, China
Yard no:	RO123-3
Engines:	4 x Sulzer 8ZAL40S
Service Speed (knots):	22.5
Flag:	Sweden
IMO Number:	9227259
Call Sign:	SBJP
Operator:	Transfennica, Finland

STENA FORETELLER

Nick Widdows

Gross Tons	24688
Net:	7407
Deadweight:	12300
Length (m):	195.3
Breadth (m):	26.8
Draught (m):	6.6
Passengers:	12
Freight:	210 trailers (13.5m)
Year built:	2002
Builders:	Dalian Shipyard, Dalian, China
Yard no:	RO123-1
Engines:	4 x Sulzer 8ZAL40S
Service Speed (knots):	22.5
Flag:	Sweden
IMO Number:	9214666
Call Sign:	SHXQ
Operator:	StoraEnso, Sweden

STENA BULK AND CONCORDIA MARITIME

STENA BULK is a leading international tanker shipping company. Stena Bulk provides both companies in the Stena sphere and external customers with marketing, chartering and commercial operations services.

Address: Stena Bulk HQ , Masthuggskajen, 405 19 Gothenburg, Sweden

Tel: +46 31 85 50 00   Fax: +46 31 12 06 51   Email: info@stenabulk.com

CONCORDIA MARITIME is an international tanker shipping company listed on the Stockholm Stock Exchange since 1984. The fleet, which is being expanded, consists of shallow navigating product tankers, designed to transport refined oil products.

Address: Concordia Maritime AB, 405 19 Gothenburg, Sweden

Tel: +46 31 85 50 00

VESSELS

Name	Built	GRT	DWT	Type	Remarks	Trading
Bm Bonanza	2007	56172	105377	Crude Oil Tanker	Double Hull	Europe
Cape Beira	2005	25400	40047	Chemical/Oil Products Tanker	Double Hull	Americas
Da Ming Hu	2003	84855	159149	Crude Oil Tanker	Double Hull	Atlantic
Da Yuan Hu	2004	84855	159149	Crude Oil Tanker	Double Hull	Atlantic
Euronike	2005	85431	164608	Oil Products Tanker	Double Hull	Atlantic
FR8 Endurance	2007	30042	50000	Chemical/Oil Products Tanker	Double Hull	Americas
Hrvatska	2005	84315	166739	Crude Oil Tanker	Double Hull	Atlantic
Ligovsky Prospect	2003	62586	114597	Crude Oil Tanker	Ice Class 1C	Europe
Mare Nostrum	2009	59611	110295	Crude Oil Tanker	Double Hull	Europe
Mare Oriens	2008	59611	110295	Crude Oil Tanker	Double Hull	Europe
Navion Gothenburg	2007	82650	152000	Crude Oil Tanker	DP Class	Employed
Nevskiy Prospect	2003	62586	114597	Crude Oil Tanker	Ice Class 1B	Europe
Nordic Cosmos	2003	81310	159999	Crude Oil Tanker	Double Hull	Atlantic
Nordic Freedom	2005	83724	159331	Crude Oil Tanker	Double Hull	Atlantic

Name	Built	GRT	DWT	Type	Remarks	Trading
Nordic Moon	2002	81310	159999	Crude Oil Tanker	Double Hull	Europe
Nordic Rio	2004	83119	152000	Crude Oil Tanker	DP Class	Employed
Nordic Voyager	1997	79494	149591	Crude Oil Tanker	Double Hull	Atlantic
Palva	2007	42810	74499	Oil Products Tanker	Ice Class 1A	Employed
Pantelis	2004	62877	114500	Crude Oil Tanker	Double Hull	Europe
Port Stewart	2003	25507	38877	Oil Products Tanker	Double Hull	Employed
Sonangol Girassol	2000	81230	149994	Crude Oil Tanker	Double Hull	Atlantic
Sonangol Kassanje	2005	83469	158706	Crude Oil Tanker	Double Hull	Atlantic
Sonangol Kizomba	2001	81230	149999	Crude Oil Tanker	Double Hull	Atlantic
Sonangol Luanda	2000	81230	149999	Crude Oil Tanker	Double Hull	Atlantic
Sonangol Namibe	2007	83469	149999	Crude Oil Tanker	Double Hull	Atlantic
Stena Alexita	1998	77440	127535	Crude Oil Tanker	DP Class II	Employed
Stena Antarctica	2006	61371	113600	Crude Oil Tanker	Ice Class 1A	Europe
Stena Arctica	2005	65293	117099	Oil Products Tanker	Ice Class 1A Super	Europe
Stena Atlantica	2006	61371	113600	Crude Oil Tanker	Ice Class 1A	Europe
Stena Calypso	2002	8613	9996	Chemical/Oil Products Tanker	C-MAX	Employed
Stena Caribbean	2002	8613	9996	Chemical/Oil Products Tanker	C-MAX	Employed
Stena Companion	2004	41589	72768	Oil Products Tanker	Double Hull/Coated	Americas
Stena Compass	2006	41589	72600	Oil Products Tanker	Double Hull/Coated	Americas
Stena Compassion	2006	41589	72600	Oil Products Tanker	Double Hull/Coated	Americas
Stena Compatriot	2004	41596	72736	Oil Products Tanker	Double Hull/Coated	Americas
Stena Concept	2005	27357	47400	Oil Products Tanker	S-47 Class	Americas
Stena Concert	2004	27463	47323	Chemical/Oil Products Tanker	Double Hull	Americas
Stena Concertina	1992	52048	96883	Crude Oil Tanker	Double Hull	Europe
Stena Concord	2004	27357	47400	Oil Products Tanker	S-47 Class	Americas
Stena Conqueror	2003	27335	47400	Chemical/Oil Products Tanker	S-47 Class	Americas

Name	Built	GRT	DWT	Type	Remarks	Trading
Stena Conquest	2003	27463	47400	Chemical/Oil Products Tanker	S-47 Class	Americas
Stena Consul	2004	27357	47400	Oil Products Tanker	S-47 Class	Americas
Stena Contest	2005	27357	47400	Oil Products Tanker	S-47 Class	Americas
Stena Fr8 1	2007	29597	50546	Chemical/Oil Products Tanker	Double Hull	Americas
Stena Fr8 2	2007	29597	50546	Chemical/Oil Products Tanker	Double Hull	Americas
Stena Natalita	2001	62393	108073	Crude Oil Tanker	DP Class II	Employed
Stena Paris	2005	36064	65125	Oil Products Tanker	P-MAX Ice Class 1B	Employed
Stena Penguin	2010	36168	65200	Oil Products Tanker	P-MAX Ice Class 1A	Europe
Stena Performance	2006	36168	65200	Oil Products Tanker	P-MAX Ice Class 1B	Employed
Stena Perros	2008	36168	65200	Oil Products Tanker	P-MAX Ice Class 1B	Europe
Stena Polaris	2009	36168	65200	Oil Products Tanker	P-MAX Ice Class 1A	Europe
Stena Poseidon	2006	42810	74499	Oil Products Tanker	Ice Class 1A	Employed
Stena Premium	2010	36168	65200	Oil Products Tanker	P-MAX Ice Class 1B	Europe
Stena President	2007	36168	65200	Oil Products Tanker	P-MAX Ice Class 1B	Employed
Stena Primorsk	2006	36168	65200	Oil Products Tanker	P-MAX Ice Class 1B	Employed
Stena Progress	2009	36168	65200	Oil Products Tanker	P-MAX Ice Class 1B	Europe
Stena Provence	2006	36168	65125	Oil Products Tanker	P-MAX Ice Class 1B	Employed
Stena Sirita	1999	77410	126671	Crude Oil Tanker	DP Class II	Employed
Stena Spirit	2001	83120	149995	Crude Oil Tanker	DP Class	Employed
Stena Tiger	2004	25400	40000	Chemical/Oil Products Tanker	Double Hull	Europe
Stena Victory	2001	163761	312638	Crude Oil Tanker	V-MAX	Employed
Stena Vision	2001	163761	312679	Crude Oil Tanker	V-MAX	Employed
Taman	1996	26218	40818	Chemical/Oil Products Tanker	Double Hull	Americas
Troitsk	1996	26218	40816	Chemical/Oil Products Tanker	Double Hull	Americas